ANGELA M. J. T

EGYPTIAN MODELS AND SCENES

SHIRE EGYPTOLOGY

Cover
A wooden kitchen model depicting the three basic food-producing activities:
baking, brewing and butchering. From tomb 585 at Beni Hasan. Middle Kingdom.
(Courtesy of Museums and Galleries on Merseyside. Liverpool Museum 55.82.7.)

British Library Cataloguing in Publication Data
Tooley, Angela M. J.
Egyptian Models and Scenes.
– (Shire Egyptology Series)
I. Title II. Series 932
ISBN 0-7478-0285-8

To my family, Eve, Beth, David and Robert, I dedicate this book.

Published by
SHIRE PUBLICATIONS LTD
Cromwell House, Church Street, Princes Risborough,
Buckinghamshire HP27 9AA, UK.

Series Editor: Barbara Adams.

ISBN 0 7478 0285 8.

First published 1995.

Printed in Great Britain by
CIT Printing Services, Press Buildings,
Merlins Bridge, Haverfordwest, Dyfed SA61 1XF.

Contents

Acknowledgements

I owe a particular debt of gratitude to Aidan Dodson, Penny Wilson and
Sara Orel for their helpful suggestions and for taking photographs for
me. Thanks are due to Sue D'Auria of the Museum of Fine Arts, Boston;
Marsha Hill of the Metropolitan Museum of Art, New York; Mogens
Jørgensen of Ny Carlsberg Glyptotèk, Copenhagen; Dagmar Winzer
and Bettina Schmitz of the Pelizaeus-Museum, Hildesheim; Renate
Krauspe of the Karl-Marx-Universität Museum, Leipzig; Vivian Davies
and John Taylor of the British Museum; John Larson of the Oriental
Institute, Chicago; Luc Limme of the Musées Royaux d'Art et d'Histoire,
Brussels; Piotr Bienkowski of the Liverpool Museum; Helen Whitehouse
of the Ashmolean Museum, Oxford; and Rosalie David of the Manchester
Museum for their help with information and photographs. I am indebted
to Professor Shore and Pat Winker of the University of Liverpool for
making the Beni Hasan photographic archive available to me at a
moment's notice and for permission to publish some of it here.
Acknowledgement is made to W. J. Murnane and Penguin Books for
the use of the dynastic chronology. Finally, thanks go to Barbara Adams
for her encouragement and help and to Jackie Fearn of Shire Publications.
Line drawings and photographs are by the author unless otherwise stated.

4

List of illustrations

Chronology

From W. J. Murnane, *The Penguin Guide to Ancient Egypt*, 1983, with names of pharaohs mentioned in the text.

Predynastic	5500-3050 BC		
		5500-4000	Badarian
		4000-3500	Naqada I (Amratian)
		3500-3200	Naqada II (Gerzean)
Protodynastic	3200-3050 BC		Naqada III/ Dynasty 0 *Narmer*
Early Dynastic/ Archaic Period	3050-2613 BC		
		3050-2890	Dynasty I *Horus Djer*
		2890-2613	Dynasties II to III
Old Kingdom	2613-2181 BC		
		2613-2498	Dynasty IV
		2558-2532	*Khaefre*
		2498-2345	Dynasty V
		2345-2181	Dynasty VI
		2345-2333	*Teti*
		2278-2184	*Pepi II*
First Intermediate Period	2181-2040 BC		
		2181-2040	Dynasties VII to X
		2134-2061	Dynasty XI (1) (Theban)
		2061-2010	*Nebhepetre Mentuhotep II*

Middle Kingdom	2040-1782 BC		
		2061-1991	Dynasty XI (2) (reunified)
		2040-2010	*Nebhepetre Mentuhotep II*
		1991-1782	Dynasty XII
		1971-1926	*Sesostris I*
		1897-1878	*Sesostris II*
		1878-1841	*Sesostris III*
Second Intermediate Period	1782-1570 BC		
		1782-1650	Dynasties XIII to XIV (Egyptian)
		1663-1555	Dynasties XV to XVI (Hyksos)
		1663-1570	Dynasty XVIl
New Kingdom	1570-1070 BC		
		1570-1293	Dynasty XVIII
		1504-1450	*Tuthmosis III*
		1453-1419	*Amenophis II*
		1334-1325	*Tutankhamun*
		1293-1070	Dynasties XIX to XX
Third Intermediate Period	1070-713 BC		Dynasties XXI to XXIV
Late Period	713-332 BC		Dynasties XXV to XXX
Graeco-Roman Period	332 BC-AD 395		
		332-30	Ptolemies
		30 BC-AD 395	Roman Emperors

1
Introduction

After the death of the body, the ancient Egyptians believed that the corpse had to be preserved, housed and provided with all the necessities and comforts of life. The passage into the next life was fraught with dangers. To overcome these, the Egyptians employed every available means to ensure a continued existence: mummification; imperishable tombs; magic formulae; carved and painted scenes; model or dummy replicas of every piece of equipment required.

Such was the Egyptians' love of life that everything placed in the tomb was there to emulate it. The most important requirement was food. The offering formula for 'thousands of bread and beer, oxen and fowl' was written on coffins, stelae and tomb walls. Real offerings of food were brought to the tomb chapel and left in its substructure. Models of food were also made.

Substitutions in the form of statues and painted scenes (figure 1) for real things and people were believed to have magical properties. The food produced in such paintings could sustain the hungry spirit through the magic of representation. This magic is at the heart of models of all kinds, whether placed in the tomb or left as votives at temples.

Designed to replace or supplement painted scenes on tomb chapel walls, models of humans, boats and animals have been found amongst grave goods from the Predynastic Period at sites such as Abadiyeh and Naqada. In most cases the purpose of the figurines is uncertain, but others, by analogy with later servant statuettes, appear to have served the dead owner in very specific ways.

First Dynasty royal tombs at Abydos were found to have rows of small graves placed round them: in the case of King Djer there were 338. Buried in them were members of the royal household, retainers and servants interred with their king at the time of his death. Intact burials at tomb 3503 at Saqqara, dating to the time of Queen Mer-neith, were of servants with the tools of their trade.

Replacing this practice, from the late Fourth Dynasty, there developed a custom of making small stone statuettes of servants and placing them in the tomb beside those of the tomb owner. Usually only one or two figures were used, but at Giza two tombs contained more. In the mastaba of Djasha of the Fifth Dynasty were found sixteen stone servant figures, whilst the tomb of Nykau-Inpu had no fewer than twenty-six servant models, the largest known single deposit of these of the Old Kingdom.

Wood began to be used for making servant models towards the end of the Sixth Dynasty and it remained the primary material for model

1. Painted wooden panel substituting for wall decoration in the same way as models and depicting a similar range of activities. Deshasheh, tomb of Meri. Late/post Sixth Dynasty. (After Petrie, *Deshasheh 1897*, 1898, plate XXVII. Oriental Institute, Chicago 2054.)

production thereafter. Some large and complete collections of wooden models have survived. From the late/post Sixth Dynasty are the models of Nyankh-Pepi-kem from tomb A1 at Meir (figure 2), comprising seventeen scenes and nine model boats. The largest Middle Kingdom deposit was from the el-Bersha tomb of the nomarch Djehutinakht and his wife, who owned some thirty-three scenes, twelve porters and fifty-five boats. The best-known models are those of the chancellor Meket-

2. Models from the tomb of Nyankh-Pepi-kem of boats, porters and various food-processing activities, as they are displayed in Cairo. Meir, tomb A1. Late/post Sixth Dynasty. (Photograph: Penny Wilson.)

Re, who was buried at Qurna (TT280). Remarkable for their state of preservation, size and attention to detail, the twenty-four models include two representations of his garden and a unique scene of cattle inspection.

As well as models of food and servants there are models of religious objects, weapons and tools. Rituals described in the Pyramid Texts and Coffin Texts (and illustrated in the *frise d'objets* on the interiors of decorated coffins) required certain paraphernalia which are found as models, such as the *pesesh-kef* set (for the ritual 'Opening of the Mouth'), the seven sacred oils set, ritual libation jars, ewers and basins, certain replica sceptres (both royal and divine), staves, shields, battleaxes, sandals and other cultic emblems such as the mirror and *pedj-aha*. All were designed to protect the passage of the deceased into the afterlife, to protect him from all harm, that he might be reborn through the potency of their magical qualities in order that he might enjoy the food and other offerings left for him.

Substituting part or all of the offerings with models of food items, dinner services (miniature or dummy dishes and jars of pottery, alabaster and wood) and servants could have reduced the cost of burial, reduced preparation time and taken less space to store. More importantly, they ensured a continued supply in the afterlife should the real offerings cease to be made at the tomb by the living.

Placed along the desert edge, tombs have remained largely dry, which has helped to preserve wooden models. However, many of the fragile figures have suffered from termite decay and destruction at the hands of robbers (figure 3). Even stone models have not survived well: of no intrinsic value to robbers, they have often been smashed. For these reasons, groups like that of Meket-Re are important for filling in the gaps left by less well-preserved models.

3. The devastation caused by tomb robbers searching for valuables. El-Bersha, tomb of Djehutinakht. Late Eleventh or early Twelfth Dynasty. (Courtesy of the Museum of Fine Arts, Boston.)

2
Model distribution and development

Geographical distribution

It has been claimed that models took the place of carved scenes in undecorated tombs in the provinces, yet it is in decorated mastabas at Giza and Saqqara during the Fourth and Fifth Dynasties that models first become common. This Memphite tradition spread during the Sixth Dynasty to sites such as Dahshur, Meydum and Sedment.

As a result of the rise in power of local potentates towards the end of the Sixth Dynasty reign of Pepi II, late/post Sixth Dynasty and First Intermediate Period wooden models were made in the southern provincial capitals of Meir, Asyut, Thebes (at el-Khokha) and Hawawish, as far south as Aswan. Most models tend to come from Upper Egypt, from sites such as Gebelein, Hawawish, Asyut and Beni Hasan, but still appear during this period in the north, from the pyramid sites of Saqqara and Abusir.

The greatest distribution of models is found in the Middle Kingdom, up to the time of Sesostris II and III. Models have been found in great numbers at all the major nome capitals, most notably at Thebes, Asyut, Meir, el-Bersha, Beni Hasan and Sedment. They have come also from Qubbet el-Hawa in the south and from the new royal necropoleis of the Twelfth Dynasty at Lahun and Lisht, as well as the Memphite sites.

The final phase, from the time of Sesostris II and III to the end of the Middle Kingdom, is limited to only a few sites. The apparent curb on the hereditary nature of the nomarch title at this time seemingly affected all the nome capital cemeteries. Where models are found at all they appear to be concentrated at Thebes (Asasif), Qau el-Kebir, Hawawish, Rifeh, el-Bersha, Beni Hasan and Dahshur. Models which can be dated to the New Kingdom tend to come from the Theban necropolis.

Poor preservation conditions may account for the lack of model remains from the Delta region. Evidence against the proposition that there were different customs outside the Nile valley is provided by a number of crude models in clay and pottery from late Middle Kingdom tombs at Dakhleh oasis.

Tomb types

Most models have been found in shaft tombs in provincial cemeteries. The term 'shaft' tomb is used to refer to a type without a superstructure. At the bottom of the shaft are one or more chambers, usually undecorated.

Other models have come from mastaba tombs (with a built superstructure) and rock-cut tombs (with a rock-cut chapel). Both these types of tomb tend to have decorated superstructures. During the Old Kingdom and Twelfth Dynasty court officials were interred in mastabas ranged round the royal pyramid, such as at Giza or Lisht. Provincial cemeteries of the late/post Sixth Dynasty and later comprise terraces of the rock-cut tombs of the nobility with, ranged below them in the foothills, the shaft tombs of lesser officials and professionals, such as at Meir, el-Bersha or Beni Hasan.

Even simpler is the pit tomb, without any chamber at the bottom of the shaft. This type of tomb was rarely used for burials of sufficient status to merit the inclusion of servant models. An exception, however, is Riqqeh 123A, which contained a boat. Pit tombs sometimes yield pottery models of agricultural implements, reflecting the agrarian nature of the population using the cemetery, such as at Esna, Mostagedda or Matmar.

Position in the tomb

Some models, usually boats, were buried in the ground outside the tomb. Examples of this are the boats found next to the pyramid of Queen Neith (wife of Pepi II) at Saqqara, and those left at the mouth of the burial shaft in the Fifth Dynasty tomb of Kaemsenu, near the pyramid of Teti. At Lisht, between the east façade and the enclosure wall of the mastaba of Djehuty, was a floor niche containing models, while four large boats were buried in the floor next to the enclosure wall of the mastaba of Imhotep. Both tombs date to the Twelfth Dynasty.

Stone servant figures and some early wooden examples were placed in the statue niche or *serdab* of Old Kingdom mastaba chapels alongside figures of the tomb owner. Models were left in the chapel of the rock-cut family tomb of Nakhti at Asyut (tomb 7), which dates to the Middle Kingdom. The majority of rock-cut tombs have been so badly disturbed that it is now impossible to know how frequently such material was left in the tomb chapel.

Other tombs containing models left above ground have them secreted in special paved-over niches cut into the floor. About halfway along the hallway in the rock-cut tomb of Meket-Re at Thebes (Qurna), a *serdab* was cut into the floor, extending under the north wall (figure 4). Into this small, 3 metre square area were packed all his fine models. In the antechamber and hallway of his sepulchre at Deir el-Bahri, King Nebhepetre Mentuhotep II had floor niches containing many wooden models.

Some models left in the shaft were placed in a specially cut *serdab*, but in the late/post Sixth Dynasty tomb of Mery-Re-khashtef at Sedment (tomb 274) the models were found buried 3 metres down in the shaft fill, lying in the south-east corner facing north.

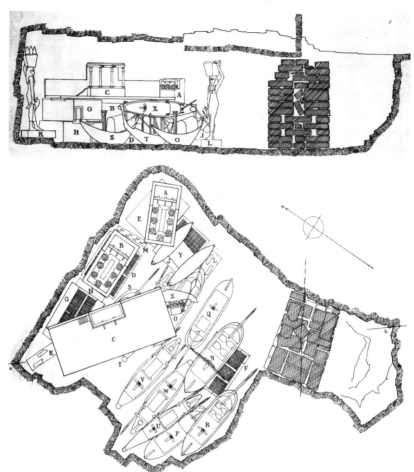

4. Section and plan of the floor niche containing Meket-Re's models. Qurna, TT 280. Late Eleventh or early Twelfth Dynasty. (From Winlock, *Models of Daily Life*, 1955, plate 55. Courtesy of the Metropolitan Museum of Art, New York.)

Models placed within the burial chamber were positioned according to the dictates of chamber size. Usually the chamber was large enough only to accommodate the coffin and a few offerings. Ideally, all offerings were placed to the left of the coffin, to be directly next to the eye panel and false door of the coffin through which the soul of the deceased could pass to partake of them. In practice, however, models have been found in all parts of the chamber; on its floor (figure 5), on the coffin lid (figure 6), and in both places (figure 7).

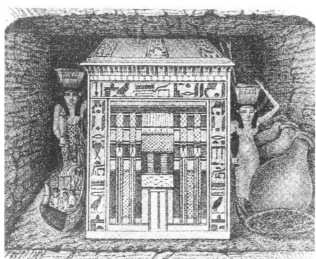

5. The scene upon opening the tomb of Mentuhotep. All the offerings, including models and pottery are placed either side of the coffin. Asasif, cemetery 600. Twelfth Dynasty. (From Schmidt, *Sarkofager, Mumiekister, og Mumiehylstre i det Gamle Aegypten. Typologisk Atlas,* 1919, figure 344.)

6. (Left) In this narrow chamber there was sufficient room only to place the models on the coffin lid. Beni Hasan, tomb 500. Twelfth Dynasty. (Courtesy of the School of Archaeology, Classics and Oriental Studies, University of Liverpool.)

7. (Right) The ceiling of the burial chamber is sufficiently high to allow the admission of the granary model on to the coffin lid. Other models are placed on the floor. Beni Hasan, tomb 1. First Intermediate Period. (Courtesy of the School of Archaeology, Classics and Oriental Studies, University of Liverpool.)

At Sedment, especially, *serdabs* were cut into the east wall of Middle
Kingdom burial chambers to accommodate the models. This was not a
new phenomenon. Tomb 223, of late Sixth Dynasty date in the Teti
cemetery at Saqqara, had a similar niche. The late/post Sixth Dynasty
tomb of Nyankh-Pepi-kem at Meir had the models placed in a paved-
over floor niche in the burial chamber, in a position below the coffin
usually associated with the canopic box.

Development

Models and scenes have their own 'cultural' chronology. There is a
cultural break with the Old Kingdom near the end of the Sixth Dynasty
(called here the late/post Sixth Dynasty), which lasts into the subsequent
dynasties but does not warrant inclusion with the First Intermediate
Period (here as the Eighth and Ninth Dynasties). Similarly, the Middle
Kingdom, in terms of models, here refers not only to the Eleventh and
Twelfth Dynasties but also to the Herakleopolitan Period (the Ninth and
Tenth dynasties, which are culturally identical).

Predynastic and Archaic Periods

Predynastic precursors of dynastic models in clay and ivory have
come from sites such as Naqada, Abadiyeh, el-Adaima, Abu Zeidan,
Kom el-Ahmar (Hierakonpolis) and el-Amrah. All the figures are crudely
made but, by comparing them with later models, their tasks can be
identified: brewers preparing beer mash, porters with hollowed-out heads
(either singly or in a row), model boats and granaries, house and town
structures, and beds.

Old Kingdom

Models of the Fourth and Fifth Dynasties are of single figures in
stone, except for the isolated instances of wooden boats. They are
generally small-scale and poorly proportioned.

The earliest Old Kingdom human servant figures are from the tombs of
Queens Meresankh III and Khamerernebti, dating to the reign of Khaefre.
This phase is restricted to activities of food preparation: milling grain,
forming dough into cakes, making beer, sifting flour and butchering a calf.
Fifth Dynasty models are of the same types with additional activities:
cleaning the interiors of jars, stoking ovens and various other tasks involved
with cooking and brewing, grain storage, and the manufacture of pottery
and metal goods. Servants carrying loads are always male. Harpist models
also appear. Boats of wood were deposited in flotillas.

Late Old Kingdom

Sometime during the Sixth Dynasty wood began to be used for servant figures, perhaps as the result of wider distribution and the need for a cheaper material than stone. Side by side with wooden figures are some elements in stone, such as braziers and jars, in composite scenes. Some late Sixth Dynasty models continued to be made in stone and were small and coarsely made, such as those from the mastabas at Kom ed-Dara. Whilst the emphasis remained on the provision of food and drink, most tombs containing models included a pair of boats and a female porter. Servant figures were now often in pairs or in small groups of allied processes, such as milling and brewing, baking and cooking. The only servant type to remain primarily single is that of the female porter.

Agriculture, in the form of cattle husbandry and men hoeing, appears, whilst the butchers and granaries of the Fifth Dynasty disappear until the First Intermediate Period and Middle Kingdom.

First Intermediate Period

The First Intermediate Period is poorly defined in terms of the model repertoire. Eighth and Ninth Dynasty models include groups of figures on a single wooden base, often a simple plank, making bread and beer; pairs of boats; and a square granary structure – the types of models typical during the Middle Kingdom.

Middle Kingdom

The greatest numbers of models and scenes were made during the Middle Kingdom. Nearly all models are of wood and in the form of groups of figures on a single base, sometimes enclosed by a low wall or entirely enclosed, as is the case with the Meket-Re models. Culturally, there are three broad phases: Ninth/Tenth Dynasty to early Eleventh Dynasty; Late Eleventh Dynasty to Sesostris II and III; post Sesostris II and III. The point of greatest diversification is the second phase. At this time, beside the usual models of boats, granary, female porter and combined food-processing scenes, there are models depicting the manufacture of goods: carpentry, weaving, brickmaking, pot making, lapidary and metalworking. Agricultural activities widen to encompass ploughing and the force-feeding, inspection and herding of cattle. Reflecting the civil unrest of the early Middle Kingdom phase and the transition between the Eleventh and Twelfth Dynasties are models of soldiers on foot and in boats.

The late Middle Kingdom phase sees a marked decline in the number and types of models, with a return to the repertoire of the First Intermediate Period of boats, female porter, granary and combined kitchen scenes.

Later models

After the end of the Middle Kingdom models decline in number. The tomb of Tutankhamun of the Eighteenth Dynasty contained several boat models, a granary and quernstone, as well as numerous model tools. Other New Kingdom deposits have also yielded boats. Models of houses, beds and chairs are known.

Figures of servants carrying offerings are limited to a series of fine wooden figures holding cosmetic jars and, in the Late Period, to coarse figures in faience and bronze bringing jars and boxes.

Figures of servants in the guise of Isis and Nephthys as mourners appear in various forms from the late New Kingdom to the Roman Period. A curious mixture of servant figure and shabti is seen in a small number of mid Eighteenth Dynasty millers.

Shabti figures may have developed from mummiform figures found on Twelfth Dynasty model boats (figure 8). Taking over some of the functions of models and scenes, true shabtis, each complete with chapter VI of the Book of the Dead inscribed on them, do not appear until the New Kingdom. During the Twelfth Dynasty early shabti types, mummiform figures and model scenes existed side by side.

8. Wooden mummiform figures resembling shabtis, from model funerary boats. Beni Hasan. Middle Kingdom. (Courtesy of the School of Archaeology, Classics and Oriental Studies, University of Liverpool.)

3
Masters, servants and offering bearers

Model owners

Tombs containing models belonged to the titled classes of Egyptian society, people who held positions of authority in state and local administration. At the head of society were the king and the royal family. Models have been found in the royal tombs of kings and queens from the Old to New Kingdoms.

Secular and religious professionals whose tombs contained models are represented by those attached to court and local administration, from the level of nomarch to overseers of various offices and stores, and secretarial staff. Persons with purely religious titles owning models are few in comparison with those bearing administrative or professional titles.

Models found in tombs where the owner appears to have had no titles on his or her coffin and possessions may indicate that the person was related by marriage or birth to a person of rank. For instance, while the daughter of a king has a recognised title, the daughter of an overseer of an estate does not. If she were buried by herself she would be without a title but nonetheless belong to the titled class.

There are, however, no set rules. Wah, steward to Meket-Re, who was buried near to his employer and whose tomb was found intact, was buried without a single servant model, yet his body was bedecked with items of real and dummy jewellery.

The owners of models made of pottery or clay – offering trays, soul houses, agricultural and domestic implements – tend to be those members of society who made up the labouring and lower classes, without sufficient wealth to construct and equip a tomb other than a simple pit.

The servants

It has been suggested that the number and type of stone models deposited in Old Kingdom tombs reflected the true size and make-up of the tomb owner's real staff. The discrepancy between those tombs where a great number have been found and the majority, which contained only two or three figures, would seem to make this unlikely. During the First Intermediate Period and Middle Kingdom, particularly, models seem to represent the ideal of an estate and the standard of living expected by the owner rather than the true number and type of servants he employed during life.

Some Old Kingdom stone servant figures have inscriptions on their bases giving the name of the owner and his titles (figure 9). Relatively

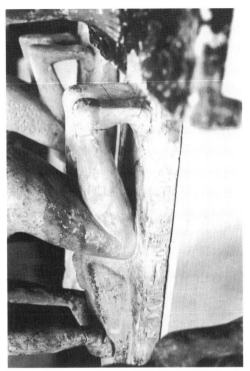

9. Inscribed base of a miller (see figure 19) reading either: 'Overseer of the Treasury, Urirni. The servant, Iat' ; or (after Fischer) 'Funerary estate of the Overseer of the Treasury, Urirni. Iat'. Saqqara, mastaba D20. Fifth Dynasty. (Cairo Museum CG 114. Photograph: Aidan Dodson.)

few are inscribed with the name of a son, a daughter or a *ka*-priest of the deceased. Others may be inscribed with the term *djet*, which can be translated as 'servant'. Some of the twenty-six figures from the Giza tomb of Nykau-Inpu are inscribed. One of them, a miller, names his daughter, Nebetempet; another, of a man making loaves, bears the name of his son, Khaef-Min (see figure 21).

It has been suggested that the designations son, daughter, *ka*-priest and servant relate to the mortuary cult of the deceased. The head of the cult or estate was the heir or son of the deceased, while the priests in his charge were his brothers and sisters. As such they were the servants of the funerary estate. The bread and beer prepared for the cult and offered at the tomb was made by real servants. Model figures of servants milling and so on are in the form of these real servants, but are inscribed with the names of the cult servants. In this way, not only did Old Kingdom models substitute for the product represented, but also for those directly responsible for the continuation of the offerings.

The majority of stone figures are not inscribed: their purpose, like the statues of the tomb owner, was explicit from their context, namely to provide the dead owner with food. Whether any of these figures can truly be said to represent a living servant is doubtful. Even those figures which are inscribed with the term *djet* may not necessarily represent a servant, since *djet* can also mean a 'funerary estate' (or its income).

A unique statue, which may be called a servant figure, depicts a kneeling man (figure 10). The base is inscribed, giving his name and title as Kaemked, *ka*-priest to Urirni, a Fifth Dynasty official buried at Saqqara. Undoubtedly of a real priest, this figure was placed among the other servant statues of Urirni.

10. (Left) Fine limestone figure of the *ka*-priest Kaemked found in the *serdab* with other stone figures of servants. Saqqara, mastaba D20. Fifth Dynasty. (Cairo Museum CG 119. From Borchardt, *Statuen und Statuetten I*, 1911, plate 26.)

11. (Above) Painted inscriptions from the bases of two porters reading: (left) 'The *imakhet*, maid servant, ... r born of Henten, justified'; (right) 'The *imakhet*, housemaid, Iki born of Dedw, justified'. Rifeh, tomb of the two brothers. Twelfth Dynasty. (Manchester Museum 4734 and 4738. After Murray, *The Tomb of the Two Brothers*, 1910, plate 17, numbers 3 and 4.)

Very few Middle Kingdom models are inscribed. Certain exceptions exist, such as the porters from the tomb of the two brothers at Rifeh (figure 11). The bases of these two figures give their position in the household, names and lineage. A similar case may be seen in the two boats of Mentuhotep buried at Asasif. The two *djerty*-mourners (see page 61) on the funerary boat of Wekhhotep from Meir are labelled with their personal names and designated 'Isis' and 'Nephthys', indicating that, like the *ka*-priest Kaemked, professionals associated with the funeral ceremony could be considered personal servants.

Other inscriptions on models are merely explanatory dockets on granary walls and scribal palettes, or part of the standard offering formula on the bases and baskets of female porters. The vast majority of servant figures and model scenes are entirely anonymous.

The bringers of offerings

Of all servants depicted in reliefs and paintings, those of men and women carrying baskets of food are the most important and are first attested on Fourth Dynasty royal monuments. Originally these figures had the physique of the god Hapy and were designated 'domains'. Later figures took on more normal proportions and were designated 'estates', in the sense of personifications of the income from mortuary estates. These latter figures were taken into the repertoire of private tomb decoration, eventually losing their formal labels in favour of the names of family or servants, and also of the offerings carried.

Model bringers of offerings, or porters, can be found singly, in pairs or in processions.

Female porters

The majority of porter models are female, usually walking, carrying a basket on the head,

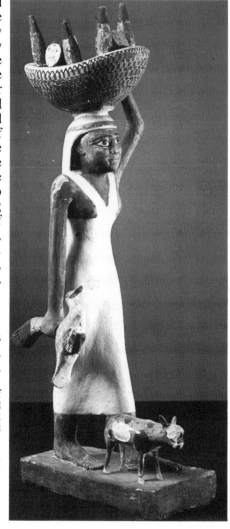

12. Painted wooden porter. Typical of early figures, she wears a wide-strapped dress and white head-cloth. The small animal in front of her may be a calf and would originally have had a linen leash. Probably from Meir, tomb of Hepi-kem. Late/post Sixth Dynasty. (Courtesy of Ny Carlsberg Glyptotèk, Copenhagen. AEIN 670.)

13. A pair of female porters standing side by side on the same base. Such pairs were frequently depicted carrying different loads, in this case a basket of provisions (right) and a pigeon or duck (left). Originally, the figure on the left also carried a large ritual libation jar. Beni Hasan, tomb 585. Late Eleventh or early Twelfth Dynasty. (Cairo Museum JE 37569.)

steadied by one hand; more offerings are held in the free hand. Such female porters first appeared as models in the late/post Sixth Dynasty in tombs from the Memphite area and south to Meir. Earlier still, models of pottery and ivory have been found in some Predynastic graves. Of simple human form, their purpose is identified by the hollowed receptacles on their heads. Old Kingdom figures occur in pairs and, in the case of Nyankh-Pepi-kem at Meir, in a group of three in descending heights (see figure 2). The porters from the mastaba of Shepi at Dahshur are a pair, although on separate bases. These early porters often have white head-cloths and carry a lidded chest on their heads.

The phenomenon of porters in pairs, either side by side or in single file, is characteristic of, although not limited to, northern sites (figure 13). The offerings in these cases are varied: for example, one woman may have a square basket and a flower, and the other a round basket and a duck.

Male porters

The very first porters which appeared as stone servant figures in the Fifth Dynasty are all male; many are given the physical characteristics of a dwarf. These figures carry beer jars or baskets of jars. A different type of porter is a youth carrying a sack over one shoulder and a pair of sandals in his hand (figure 14). This motif recalls the sandal-bearer on the Narmer palette. The nakedness of this figure indicates his status as a minor.

A particularly fine male porter of painted wood is from the tomb of Nyankh-Pepi-kem at Meir (figure 15). With a basket or satchel strapped to his back, he carries a wicker box in front of him.

Unlike female porters, male porters are never depicted in pairs but may be found as members of processions of both men and women and of men only. The offerings they carry are usually different from those brought by female porters.

14. A limestone figure of a naked male porter carrying a pair of sandals and a sack (?). Saqqara, mastaba D54. Fifth Dynasty. (Cairo Museum CG 111. From Borchardt, *Statuen und Statuetten 1*, 1911, plate 24.)

15. (Below) Wooden male porter bringing a wicker box and a satchel. Their contents are unknown. Meir, tomb of Nyankh-Pepi-kem. Late/post Sixth Dynasty. (Cairo Museum CG 241.)

16. The el-Bersha Procession as reconstructed. Led by a shaven-headed priest, the group includes a woman carrying a mirror case and jewel box. El-Bersha, tomb of Djehutinakht. Late Eleventh or early Twelfth Dynasty. (Courtesy of the Museum of Fine Arts, Boston. Object 21.326.)

Processions

Processions of porters are uncommon, known examples coming from the sites of Saqqara, Thebes, Meir and el-Bersha. The Saqqara processions are distinguished by being two files of men and women. The earlier model, possibly from the late/post Sixth Dynasty tomb of Tjeteti, originally had fourteen figures, while that of Karenen, of Middle Kingdom date, had twenty. The most famous procession is the one from the Middle Kingdom tomb of Djehutinakht at el-Bersha (figure 16). A shaven-headed priest at the front is followed by three women, each with a different hairstyle and offerings. A similar, though less accomplished, procession was found in the tomb of Meket-Re (model M).

The offerings

Whilst the contents of many baskets must be inferred, some have painted and modelled offerings in the form of cuts of meat, bread, vegetables, fruits and jars of beer. Hand-held offerings include lotus and lily blossoms, wildfowl and small antelope or calves on leashes.

17. Male porter bringing a writing board and scribal palette. El-Bersha, tomb of Djehutinakht. Late Eleventh or early Twelfth Dynasty. (Museum of Fine Arts, Boston 21.11769. Photograph: Aidan Dodson.)

As in painted scenes, male porters carry objects and equipment for the tomb such as furniture, boxes, piles of linen, sacks of grain, ritual libation jars and scribal equipment (figure 17).

Discussion

Porters, particularly female ones, had more importance than other model types. This is evident from the care with which they were made, the attention to detail and their often much larger scale. For instance, the two porters of Meket-Re (figure 18), models K and L, are the finest examples ever found and are 122 and 112 cm tall (including baskets). The el-Bersha Procession (figure 16) also is the finest of its type and much larger (41.5 cm) than other models from the same tomb. Most porters are between 30 and 60 cm tall, contrasting with an overall height of between 10 and 40 cm for group scenes. Female porters are usually made in pairs. Why this should be so is unclear but it may relate to the ideological concepts in Egyptian thought of pairs like Upper and Lower Egypt, the Red and the Black (desert and valley), order and chaos. It is possible that pairs of female porters may have been believed to represent personifications of the Two Lands (or their titular goddesses, Wadjet and Nekhbet) as well as those elements necessary for continued existence in the tomb, food and drink.

Other models which may be porters include the painted wooden figure of a woman personifying *sekhet*: a field or irrigation basin (and its produce). With the *sekhet* hieroglyph on her head, she carries wildfowl in her hands. In 1987 several female statuette fragments were found in the offering hall of the mortuary temple of Sesostris I at Lisht. One of these fragments is the upper portion of what appears to be a female personification of Hapy, recalling the two-dimensional depictions of Hapy porters, both male and female, of earlier monuments.

Implicitly, single porters provided for all the needs of the deceased, encapsulating as they do the duality of food and drink, the fecundity of the Nile god Hapy, the crops from the fields, and the income from the mortuary cult. Processions of porters simply emphasise the multiplicity of offerings required by the tomb owner throughout eternity, while at the same time giving status in the afterlife to him through the number of servants depicted in his employ.

Of all models and scenes, porters, because of their larger scale and better construction, have recognisable artistic regional styles. For instance, as a general guide, female porters from Asyut may have polychrome ornamented dresses and/or pigtails. Theban figures tend to be

larger than those from elsewhere, being tall and slender with high jutting hip bones, and sometimes a green dress. Beni Hasan porters are characterised by their rather crude appearance and angular, down-curved mouths. Carried offerings often include a brace of wildfowl. Sedment porters are usually in pairs on a shared base board and are virtually stick figures.

18. The finest porters ever found are from the tomb of Meket-Re. Half life-size, the figures wear colourful dresses and carry beer jars and food offerings. Qurna, models K and L. Late Eleventh or early Twelfth Dynasty. (Left: Cairo Museum JE 46725. Right: New York 20.3.7. From Winlock, *Models of Daily Life*, 1955, plate 30. Courtesy of the Metropolitan Museum of Art, New York. Photography by the Egyptian Expedition, the Metropolitan Museum of Art, New York.)

4
Kitchens, granaries and storehouses

Baking

Egyptian bread was made from the flour of emmer wheat, but some special varieties used for offerings were made from barley. The Meket-Re bakery (model G) depicts all the stages from grain to bread, although most models are not so detailed and show only the basic processes. Old Kingdom models of single figures each show one stage.

The bakery processes comprised pounding the grains in a mortar, grinding them into flour on a quern, sifting the flour, making dough, shaping it into loaves and baking in an oven.

The most common Old Kingdom servant figures are those of millers. They are usually female. In Meket-Re's bakery, of all the workers shown it is only the millers who are female. Kneeling over quernstones, they have short hair, which may be covered by a protective cloth to prevent hair falling into the flour and flour getting into their hair (figure 19). Post Sixth Dynasty and First Intermediate Period millers continue to kneel, while those of the Middle Kingdom usually stand at querns set in waist-high casings. The 'thrusting' hand-mill of wood and sandstone from a box in the Treasury of Tutankhamun's tomb (Carter object 279) is just such a model. A crude clay miller from a Thirteenth Dynasty burial at Qila' el-Dabba (Balat) in the Dakhleh oasis appears to sit at her quern.

19. Fine limestone miller. She wears a protective head-cloth and grinds cereals from the small sack in front of her knees. Saqqara, mastaba D20. Fifth Dynasty. (Cairo Museum CG 114. Photograph: Aidan Dodson.)

20. Small uninscribed miller, wearing the side-lock and panther skin that denotes his office as high priest in the temple of Ptah at Memphis. Limestone. Probably from Saqqara. Mid Eighteenth Dynasty. (Courtesy of Ny Carlsberg Glyptotèk, Copenhagen. AEIN 1548.)

A highly specialised type of servant figure from the New Kingdom is seen in the form of a small group of millers. Of stone or bronze and much smaller in scale than traditional millers, these figures, standing, kneeling or prostrate, belonged to high priests in the temple of Ptah at Memphis. The figures, sometimes inscribed, depict the priestly garb of panther skin, side-lock and long beard (figure 20). The shabti text inscribed on them indicates that the owners represented themselves as millers in order to make the offerings for Nut or Osiris, so that they could benefit from being in the company of the gods as their personal attendants.

Sifting flour, seen only in Old Kingdom models, is done using an either square or round basketry sieve with another basket below to catch the flour. Old Kingdom models also show servants kneading dough into loaves. Sometimes with hands white from the flour, the baker makes loaves varying in shape from round to ingot-shaped (figure 21). Baking the bread was done most often in an oven formed of stacked bread moulds with a fire lit below. The oven attendant would sit next to the stoke-hole, with a poker in one hand and the other raised to the side of the head to protect the face from the intense heat (figure 22).

From the late/post Sixth Dynasty baking and brewing activities were combined in a single scene.

Egyptian Models and Scenes

21. Limestone baker forming ingot-shaped cakes. Inscribed with the name of Khaef-Min, son of Nykau-Inpu. Probably from Giza, mastaba of Nykau-Inpu. Fifth Dynasty. (Courtesy of The Oriental Institute of The University of Chicago. Object 10624.)

22. (Below) Limestone oven attendant. She would once have held a separate poker to stoke the fire over which the bread moulds are stacked. Giza. Fifth Dynasty. (Courtesy of the Pelizaeus-Museum, Hildesheim. Inv. Nr. 2140.)

23. Painted limestone brewer pushing mash through a sieve. Giza, mastaba of Meresankh. Fifth Dynasty. (Cairo Museum JE 66624. Photograph: Aidan Dodson.)

Brewing

Egyptian beer was a thick, cloudy brew. It was made from partially cooked barley bread mixed with water, which was then strained into large vats and bottled into smaller, sealed jars.

Mashing, that is straining the fermented bread mixture (the mash) into a vat, is usually done by a brewer standing behind a waist-high vessel and pushing the mash through a wicker sieve with his hands (figure 23). Some models, including a Predynastic example from Naqada, show the brewer standing inside a vat treading the mash under foot (figure 24).

Old Kingdom models depict a brewer standing by a vessel on supports and holding a dipping cup in one hand. A

24. Wooden brewery model showing a man standing in a vat either kneading dough or pressing mash; others bring supplies of water, sieve mash and transfer beer into jars. Beni Hasan, tomb 116. Late Eleventh or early Twelfth Dynasty. (Courtesy of the School of Archaeology, Classics and Oriental Studies, University of Liverpool. Cairo Museum.)

25. Squatting limestone servant cleaning the interior of a beer jar. Saqqara, mastaba D56. Fifth Dynasty. (Cairo Museum CG 113. Photograph: Aidan Dodson.)

similar pose is adopted by one of Meket-Re's brewers, who is transferring the beer mixture from large vats to smaller jars. The final stage is to prepare the storage jars for a new batch of beer. Figures of men squatting with one hand inside a beer jar may represent a cleaning process (figure 25), although it is also possible that they are coating the interior with waterproofing pitch.

Meat products

The sacrifice and butchering of cattle is a common painted scene. The model butcher leans over a small trussed bull, poised to cut its throat with a curved flint knife (figure 26). One of the earliest Old Kingdom model

26. Limestone butcher slaughtering a bound calf (?). Giza, mastaba of Djasha. Fifth Dynasty. (Cairo Museum JE 37823. Photograph: Aidan Dodson.)

types is a butcher from the tomb of Queen Meresankh III.

Model E of Meket-Re, the abattoir, is a two-storey structure with meat cuts hanging from an upper terrace (figure 27). Below, in the courtyard, are bound bulls, their throats cut. Beside each animal is an attendant who catches the blood in large bowls. This was mixed with flour to make a kind of blood pudding and cooked in large cauldrons over an open brazier.

Other types of meat are represented being prepared. In a rare Old Kingdom servant figure from the tomb of Djasha, a man cleans the carcase of a goose or duck ready for cooking.

27. View into an abattoir in which cattle are slaughtered. Their blood is collected and cooked as a pudding in cauldrons (top left). Qurna, tomb of Meket-Re, model E. Late Eleventh or early Twelfth Dynasty. (New York 20.3.10. From Winlock, *Models of Daily Life*, 1955, plate 19 top. Courtesy of the Metropolitan Museum of Art, New York. Photography by the Egyptian Expedition, the Metropolitan Museum of Art, New York).

28. Combined model of baking (right), brewing (middle) and butchering (left) in separate rooms of a kitchen. Saqqara, tomb of Gemniemhat. Late Eleventh or early Twelfth Dynasty. Courtesy of Ny Carlsberg Glyptotèk, Copenhagen. AEIN 1631.)

Scenes of the Eleventh and Twelfth Dynasties increase in complexity, combining the activities of the baker, brewer and butcher on one base, later models tending to place these activities within separate rooms (figure 28).

Models of food

From the late Fifth Dynasty individual models of prepared poultry were made in stone. Cuts of meat predominate among models of other foods, as well as types of bread and vegetables. This type of model developed from stone food containers modelled to represent their contents. In the Middle Kingdom models of individual food items continued to be made of wood, stone, pottery, faience and cartonnage and are predominantly of fruit and vegetables.

Fishing

While fish must have featured widely in Egyptian diet they are rarely found as models. Exceptionally, model Y of Meket-Re represents two papyrus skiffs or marsh fishing boats (figure 29). Between them they drag a seine net full of different types of Nile fish. Another boat, this

29. Papyrus fishing rafts dragging a seine net between them full of different types of fish. Qurna, tomb of Meket-Re, model Y. Late Eleventh or early Twelfth Dynasty. (Cairo Museum JE 46715. Photograph: Penny Wilson.)

time a river craft (model X), has a number of men on board spearing fish with harpoons, while other people hold several brace of wildfowl, probably brought down with boomerangs. Fishing is also the subject of a small, shallow-draught boat equipped with a net from Sedment.

Cooking

An unusual model found only in the Old Kingdom is of a cook with a cauldron of small round objects (figure 30). Scenes in the tombs of Ti and Mereruka identify these as boiled bread pellets for the force-feeding of domestic fowl.

Meat was either stewed or roasted. An uncommon type of model found only during the Old Kingdom is of a man squatting next to a brazier over which is a large cooking pot full of meat cuts. A late/post Sixth Dynasty wooden model depicts a man roasting a spitted bird by hand over an open fire kept hot by the use of a feather fan (figure 31). It is uncertain whether the bird is a duck, goose or pigeon.

31. (Above) Wooden model of a servant roasting a spitted duck (?) over a brazier of hot coals. Meir, tomb of Nyankh-Pepi-kem. Late/post Sixth Dynasty. (Cairo Museum CG 245.)

30. (Left) A limestone squatting servant stirs a pot of bread pellets over a brazier. Giza, mastaba of Djasha. Fifth Dynasty. (Courtesy of the Ägyptisches Museum der Universität, Leipzig, Inv. Nr. 2526.)

Granaries

Storage was an important feature of Egyptian estates and houses. Cereal grains, bread and beer needed to be stored and kept dry during the time of annual inundation. It is not surprising, therefore, that granaries are amongst the first models to appear and that large model silos were even built and incorporated into the structures of some Archaic mastaba tombs. Two types of granary are known, domed and flat-roofed.

Domed granaries

Painted scenes in the Sixth Dynasty depict these tall domed structures on a low platform. By the end of the dynasty they were represented as vaults between tall walls resembling the *naos* hieroglyph. A wooden model of post-Sixth Dynasty date from Akhmim reflects this type of structure exactly (figure 32). Painted scenes of domed silos continued into the Middle Kingdom, when the domes are often preceded by, or interspersed with, columns. During the New Kingdom most domestic silos are shown as domed.

32. Unique wooden model of a row of painted domed silos, with movable shutters on the ground floor. Akhmim. Late/post Sixth Dynasty. (Cairo Museum JE 28839. Photograph: Sara Orel.)

The earliest models of granaries are from First Dynasty tombs at Tarkhan and Abydos. Of pottery, they are straight-sided with domed tops. On the sides are modelled windows at two levels for the extraction of grain. Other, similar jars are from the Third Dynasty step pyramid complex at Saqqara.

Amongst Old Kingdom stone models, granaries are rare. The silos are domed with a conical stopper in the top, by means of which grain was introduced; on the sides are inscribed the names of different types of cereals. The model from the tomb of Djasha (figure 33) shows a granary

33. Limestone model of a granary worker and silos. In such models the scale of buildings to humans is reversed. Giza, mastaba of Djasha. Fifth Dynasty. (Courtesy of the Ägyptisches Museum der Universität, Leipzig. Inv. Nr. 2566.)

worker filling a measuring drum with grain in front of five small silos. Of all models, this example demonstrates how structures and figures are depicted totally out of scale; the figure is shown many times larger than the structure, which would have been several storeys high.

From the Fourth Dynasty to the New Kingdom, domed models are most often made in pottery. The earlier models (figure 34) resemble their stone counterparts. Second Intermediate Period and Eighteenth

34. Pottery granary comprising twelve domed silos with conical stoppers. El-Kab, mastaba A. Fourth Dynasty. (Courtesy of the Visitors of the Ashmolean Museum, Oxford. E. 408.)

35. Single dome granary or beehive pot. The doorway is cut out of the side of the pot and would once have been closed with a separate door (missing). Esna. Second Intermediate Period. (University of Liverpool E4292.)

Dynasty models (figure 35) are made from upturned pots with a window and separate door, sometimes called beehive pots because of their shape.

A unique Middle Kingdom pottery granary from Salmiya has two storeys of grain bins. Those on the upper level are domed and painted grey to simulate the brick from which real silos were built. The figures of the owner, the scribe and granary workers are painted on the sides of the model rather than being modelled in the round, as in wooden granaries. Like this model, some pottery soul houses (see chapter 6) have domed silos modelled on their roofs.

Flat-roofed granaries

The hieroglyph or ideogram for granary in Egyptian is *shenut*. It depicts an enclosure wall with peaked corners, within which is a flat-

36. Typical wooden model granary with slightly peaked walls, painted shutters and holes in the terrace through which grain was introduced into the bins. Sedment, tomb 374. Late Eleventh or early Twelfth Dynasty. (Musées Royaux d'Art et d'Histoire, Brussels. E.5798c.)

topped pile of grain. This type of structure most closely resembles New Kingdom royal estate storage facilities shown in reliefs at Amarna. Flat-roofed granaries are rare in painted scenes, most representations coming from the tombs at Beni Hasan.

Most model granaries with flat roofs are of wood. The earliest examples of this type are from the First Intermediate Period from the sites of Gebelein and Qubbet el-Hawa (Aswan).

The majority of granaries have a simple plan (figure 36), square or rectangular; the corners of the walls may be peaked. The door may be real or painted, giving access to a courtyard. Along the back wall are the flat-roofed silos, with either painted or modelled sliding doors. To one side are stairs leading to the terrace. Workers in these models usually include a scribe, who sits on the upper terrace, a man filling a grain measure and one or two men carrying grain sacks.

37. Combined model depicting a granary (back), bakery (right) and weaving shed (front). Lisht, mastaba of Djehuty. Twelfth Dynasty. (Courtesy of the Metropolitan Museum of Art, New York, and reproduced by courtesy of Indiana University Art Museum, Bloomington. William Lowe Bryan Memorial 58.34.)

Meket-Re's granary (model F) differs from other models in its complexity. A door gives access to a court. Through a door to one side is a staircase leading on to a platform. Three bins are ranged on two walls of the enclosure. There are sixteen figures in this model, which far exceeds the number in other granary models but probably reflects more accurately the true number of staff employed in such facilities.

Some models, including that of Meket-Re, have real cereals filling the bins. Others have miniature granary sacks. Ink labels on some models indicate that they were used to store barley, spelt, wheat, green corn, white corn, dura, as well as figs, dates, raisins and a range of other unidentified fruits; sometimes capacity is also marked. Baking and brewing may also be represented in the courtyard. It is because the activities of these model types are so closely allied that a granary was incorporated with a kitchen scene in a model from Lisht (figure 37).

38. Side view into Tutankhamun's model granary (the door is to the left). Thebes, KV 62, Carter object 277. Eighteenth Dynasty. (Cairo Museum. Photograph: Aidan Dodson.)

The only granary structure later than the Middle Kingdom is the large, white-painted and gilded wooden model from the tomb of Tutankhamun (figure 38, Carter object 277). Enclosed by a buttressed wall, the small, centrally placed door opens on to sixteen compartments filled to the top with grains that include barley and emmer wheat.

A series of pottery models from Beni Hasan are of flat-roofed granaries,

39. Detailed granary model with workers, an overseer, several scribes and a covered canopy for them to sit under. El-Bersha, tomb of Sepi III. Twelfth Dynasty. (Cairo Museum JE 32831.)

with open-air storage bins. They do not seem to have had either modelled or painted figures.

Archaeological evidence for granaries

The archaeological evidence for granaries is not easy to reconcile with that provided by models. Granary structures from settlement sites like Deir el-Medina, Amarna and Gurob are usually circular and domed.

The closest parallel for flat-roofed Middle Kingdom wooden models comes from a granary found by Petrie at Kahun. Square in plan, it had a covered colonnade, with a bench for the scribes opposite three large silos, cellars and storage pits. The Second Cataract forts and some large houses at Kahun also had rectilinear granaries. One model from el-Bersha (figure 39) very closely resembles the Kahun structure.

The difference in construction between flat-roofed and domed models may be that the former represents large scale storage on estates, while the latter is for domestic storage. This point remains unclear, however.

Storehouses

Like the abattoir model of Meket-Re, storehouses are usually enclosed by a high wall, roofed at the back over a pillared terrace (figure 40). The figures in the courtyard engage in baking, brewing and butchering. One or more doors in the back wall lead to storage facilities for grain and other produce, as in a granary, while the upper terrace accommodates lines on which hang cuts of meat. Storehouses encapsulate the whole gamut of food production and storage, from cereal grains to cooked meat.

40. Storehouse model with a covered upper terrace. In the courtyard men are baking and brewing. On the terrace are model meat cuts which once hung from a line. Saqqara, tomb of Karenen. Late Eleventh or early Twelfth Dynasty. (Cairo Museum temporary register 14/3/15/8. Photograph: Aidan Dodson.)

5
Industry and agriculture

Carpentry shops

Model J of Meket-Re is the most detailed of all carpentry scenes. In the workshop men cut and shape wood using copper tools such as saws, axes, chisels and adzes and smooth it with abrasive stones. A plank lashed to a vertical post is cut into thinner sections with a pull saw. Three men at the back of the shop boost the heat in a small forge through blowpipes, probably to re-temper old tools. A supply of new model tools and spare metal blades was placed inside a sealed box within the carpentry shop.

41. Carpenters using a 'pull' saw and adze (missing). El-Bersha, tomb of Djehutinakht. Late Eleventh or early Twelfth Dynasty. (Museum of Fine Arts, Boston 21.412. Photograph: Aidan Dodson.)

Carpentry shops are otherwise rare, examples coming from the tombs of Djehutinakht at el-Bersha (figure 41) and Karenen, User-Mut and Gemniemhat at Saqqara. In the Saqqara models the activity is combined with other manufacturing processes. Miniature carpentry tools (figure 42) have been found in tombs from the Old Kingdom, and a great many dating to the Middle Kingdom from Sedment and Beni Hasan, often inside small cloth bags. The sets comprise chisels, awls, adzes, axes and saws. In Egyptian belief tools without an accompanying manufacturing scene functioned in the same manner to produce any item that was required.

Workshops

The earliest example of a model showing pottery production is a figure from the Nykau-Inpu group. This Fifth Dynasty model shows an emaciated man squatting before a low potter's wheel (at this date, a slow wheel), which he turns with one hand while forming a bowl with the other. Beside him are three finished jars.

42. Factory model combining carpentry (back left) and metalworking (back right) with pottery making (front). With the workshop was a spare set of carpenters' tools. Saqqara, tomb of Gemniemhat. Late Eleventh or early Twelfth Dynasty. (Courtesy of Ny Carlsberg Glyptotèk, Copenhagen. AEIN 1633.)

Pottery making is rarely shown in wooden models. Dating to the Middle Kingdom, models from Saqqara combine carpentry, pottery making and metalworking, with the addition of lapidary in one model. The potters in these models prepare the balls of clay and form pots on slow wheels behind which they squat (figure 42). Karenen's model shows the large cylindrical kiln in which the thrown pots were to be fired. It is unclear whether the potters found in the tomb of Nebhepetre Mentuhotep II came from workshops or single-activity models.

Rarer still than potters are those models showing the production of metal objects. A figure from the Nykau-Inpu group, of the Fifth Dynasty, depicts a man blowing through a pipe into a small forge. He is shown as a hunchback, illustrating that minor figures could be portrayed with physical deformities – unlike their masters.

Metalworking is shown in only two Middle Kingdom models, excluding those in the Meket-Re carpentry shop. The more detailed model is from the tomb of Gemniemhat at Saqqara (figure 42). It shows two men providing the draught for a forge through blowpipes, while the crucible for the molten metal stands in readiness nearby on a wooden box.

An apparently unique bronze statuette of uncertain date, in the Fitzwilliam Museum (E.2.1993), appears to show a squatting smith with a cylindrical hammer stone and an axe blade held between tongs.

The production of stone vessels is found with certainty only once. The workshop of User-Mut includes a single figure hollowing a jar with a bow drill and sand abrasive, kept in a bowl beside him. The purpose of all these models was to provide a supply of consumables: jars, tools and joinery.

Brickmaking
    Two models that depict the production of bricks belonged to Djehutinakht of el-Bersha. They show men mixing mud, water and other ingredients with a hoe and transporting the mixture on a carrying pole to a man who puts the mud into a mould. In front of him are rows of finished bricks, indicated by scored lines painted black. A similar, smaller model is from tomb 275 at Beni Hasan (figure 43). The provision of bricks would enable the tomb owner to perpetuate the buildings on his estate – the workshops, sheds, granaries and houses – and even allow the building of new structures.

43. Model of men making bricks. Two men mix the mud, while a third presses the mixture into a brick mould. Beni Hasan, tomb 275. Eleventh Dynasty. (Courtesy of the British Museum, London.   EA 63837.)

Spinning and weaving sheds
    Of all the manufacturing processes, the production of cloth is most often depicted. In the standard offering formula found on coffins, stelae and other objects, cloth appears after offerings of food and fine stone, indicating its importance in Egyptian life.
    Ten or so models, all Middle Kingdom, are known to depict spinning and weaving. Excepting models from Sedment and Beni Hasan, they all show the activity taking place inside a walled shed. The figures are exclusively female, as in painted scenes: only women are shown making linen cloth on horizontal looms until the beginning of the New Kingdom.

44. View into a spinning and weaving shed. Qurna, tomb of Meket-Re, model H. Late Eleventh or early Twelfth Dynasty. (Cairo Museum JE 46723. Photograph: Aidan Dodson.)

Meket-Re's model H (figure 44) depicts groups of women making roves of twisted flax fibres, some wound into balls, ready for the spinners. Two of the spinners stand with one leg raised on which to roll their spindles. Other women wrap finished thread on to pegs in the walls to produce warp threads for the next loom. The two horizontal looms being worked are made from pieces of wood painted in imitation of warp and weft threads.

Most models are far simpler, with only one or two spinners and weavers and a loom painted on to the model base. Djehutinakht's model has four pegs and two rods around which real linen threads were originally wound to make the loom.

That weaving, at least sometimes, took place indoors is indicated by the roof on Meket-Re's model and by the vaulted structures over all the Saqqara models. In some instances these vaulted models were found in poor condition or lacking their figures. In error, the vaults were interpreted as vineyards for training vines. Complete models indicate that this is not so. In Egyptian society fine linen distinguished the wealthy from the labouring classes. The inclusion of models of spinning and weaving sheds in the tombs of the nobility ensured a supply of fine linen clothing.

Shoemaking

A single model from Beni Hasan (tomb 275) shows a worker squatting before two roughly shaped objects, with a knife in his hand (figure 45). The shapes resemble the soles of sandals cut from a piece of leather. On the whole, only gods and persons of high status wore sandals. Burials of the First Intermediate Period and Middle Kingdom often include amongst the offerings a pair of model wooden sandals.

45. Model shoemaker cutting sandal soles from leather (?). Beni Hasan, tomb 275. Eleventh Dynasty. (Courtesy of the School of Archaeology, Classics and Oriental Studies, University of Liverpool.)

Launderette

Two or three models, all from the Saqqara necropolis, depict a curious activity (figure 46), the purpose of which is disputed. They show figures beating with a club, while others pull on horizontal rods originally attached to a vertical post in the ground.

Two possibilities present themselves. Painted scenes in the New Kingdom tomb of Khaewase show similar poses and appear to depict the beating and twisting of flax or papyrus into lengths of rope. Alternatively, beating and twisting is part of the laundering process, as depicted in the Middle Kingdom tomb of Khnum-hotep at Beni Hasan. The models, in addition, show men with what appear to be folded white objects on their heads: perhaps freshly laundered sheets.

46. Model launderette. The sheets are cleaned by beating and dried by twisting on rods. The figure walking away from the scene carries on his head freshly laundered linen, and carries in his hands a beating board and club. Saqqara, tomb of User-Mut and Inpu-emhat. Late Eleventh or early Twelfth Dynasty. (Cairo Museum JE 46765. Photograph: Aidan Dodson.)

47. Model of a farm labourer with a hoe. Asyut. Middle
Kingdom. (British Museum, London. EA 45195.)

One of the figures on the launderette model
from the burial of Nefersemdet (wife of
Karenen) has about his waist a belt,
suspended from which are a pouch and tools
interpreted as the equipment of a barber-
surgeon.

Agriculture

While paintings and reliefs illustrate
virtually every aspect of cereal cultivation
from hoeing to harvesting, models are limited
in scope. A series of models depicting
cultivation comes from Middle Egypt, the
region of Asyut to Beni Hasan.

Preparing the soil for sowing was done
initially with a hoe (figure 47). This model
type is first found amongst the late/post Sixth
Dynasty models of Nyankh-Pepi-kem. Ploughing the fields was done
with a wooden plough dragged by cattle (figure 48). The plough drivers
and hoers are depicted without feet, an indication that they are wading
through freshly turned, moist soil. Even though cultivation is essential
before the processing of grain into flour, it did not figure largely in the
model repertoire.

Agricultural tools appear as clay models in cemeteries where wooden

48. A pair of cattle pull a plough, urged on by a man wielding a stick. In such models there is
sometimes a third figure who broadcasts seeds from a basket. Provenance unknown. Twelfth
Dynasty (?). (Courtesy of the British Museum, London. EA 51090.)

49. Model of a man force-feeding a long-horned bull. El-Bersha, tomb of Djehutinakht. Late Eleventh or early Twelfth Dynasty. (Museum of Fine Arts, Boston 21.823. Photograph: Aidan Dodson.)

and stone models are not found, such as at Esna. A collection of hoes, pestles, dummy vessels and sieves was found in grave 154. Agricultural implements of copper were sometimes supplied separately with shabti figures, in the form of two types of hoe, and seed baskets. Wooden model agricultural implements are also known, such as the model hoe from the tomb of Tutankhamun (Carter object 94b).

Animal husbandry

Cattle were kept primarily for their milk and cheese and their strength as draught animals. As sacrificial animals their meat was important in divine and funerary cults. Beef was not generally available to other than the wealthy nobility. Cattle husbandry appears amongst the Meket-Re models in the form of the abattoir (model E) and a stable (model D). The most imposing scene from Meket-Re's tomb is model C, that of the chancellor and his scribes sitting under a pavilion, inspecting a herd of nineteen animals driven in front of them. The number of cattle depicted gives some indication of Meket-Re's status, especially as other models of husbandry depict single animals, sometimes pairs.

Other models of cattle husbandry are limited to a few sites in Middle Egypt: Asyut, el-Bersha, Beni Hasan and Meir. This region was particularly fertile and may have had a greater number of cattle than

50. A woman milks a cow, while its calf stands nearby. Asyut. Twelfth Dynasty (?). (Courtesy of the Pelizaeus-Museum, Hildesheim. Inv. Nr. 1690.)

elsewhere in the Nile valley. This regional tendency to include essentially farming models in the tomb may indicate a greater emphasis on animal husbandry in the daily lives of those who owned them rather than an indication of wealth, as is the case with the Meket-Re models. The greater majority of models which show cattle, the butchers' shops, are an indication of the means to afford to purchase an animal for slaughter.

Models of cattle show bulls or calves either standing or lying; some are force-fed and too fat to stand and are ready for the slaughterhouse (figure 49). Other aspects of husbandry include a unique model of a cow calving and of a woman milking a cow (figure 50), said to be from Asyut.

6
Travel, home and tomb

Communication and travel in Egypt was primarily by boat. All transport of goods, materials and persons was via the Nile, along the length of the river, from town to town, from one bank to the other. Only the most local travel was by foot or using beasts of burden.

River transport

By the Middle Kingdom by far the most numerous of all models are boats. In his Cairo catalogue *Models of Ships and Boats* (1913), G. A. Reisner organised them into seven basic categories. Several other types of boats from the Old to New Kingdoms were discovered later.

Typology (figure 51)

I. Square-cut river craft with two rudders (Old Kingdom).
II. River craft with curling stern and one rudder (Middle Kingdom).
III. Papyrus raft or skiff (Predynastic Period onward).
IV. Papyriform wooden craft (Old to Middle Kingdom).
V. Papyriform wooden craft with raised end post (Archaic Period onward).
VI. Solar barques (Twelfth Dynasty).
VII. Divine barques (New Kingdom onward).

Conspicuous by their absence from this standard typology are river craft of New Kingdom date. They have a deeply curved hull profile (figure 51) and often amidships there is a cabin following the line of the deck. Also, types of Predynastic and Archaic Period models do not appear (figure 51). The typology should be noted as very general and does not take account of model construction: whether hollowed out or of solid construction.

Each type of boat was for use under different circumstances: by the living for ordinary transport (types I, II, III); for use in funerals or on symbolic pilgrimages by the dead (types IV, V, VII and sometimes II); or for highly specialised religious functions (types VI, VII). It is the equipping of model boats of all types which determines their use, from simple travel to armed escort.

Generally, two boat models were provided per tomb, one rigged for sailing, one for rowing (figure 52). Often these pairs were positioned in the tomb facing in opposite directions to emphasise the acts of sailing south with the prevailing wind and rowing north with the current of the river. Large flotillas of models have been found in some instances, consisting of pairs of different types of boats and covering most aspects

52

51. Reisner types I to VII boat model hull profiles, with Predynastic and New Kingdom types.

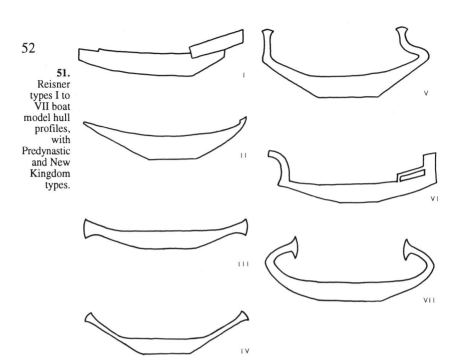

I

V

II

VI

III

VII

IV

PRE-DYNASTIC

NEW KINGDOM

52. A pair of type II boats for sailing (left) and rowing (right) placed on the coffin lid facing in different directions to emphasise their direction of travel. Beni Hasan, tomb 275. Eleventh Dynasty. (Courtesy of the School of Archaeology, Classics and Oriental Studies, University of Liverpool.)

of usage. As most models are of rough construction, it can often be difficult to distinguish craft type. This is particularly true of papyriform vessels III and IV, since one is a model of a papyrus skiff and the other is a model of a wooden imitation of a papyrus craft used for ritual purposes, such as funerals (figure 53).

53. Type IV boat with end posts painted to imitate the tied papyrus bundles of type III boats. This particular boat is unique in the use of a canopy with a square hole cut in its roof, which may have been covered by a linen screen. Beni Hasan, tomb 1. First Intermediate Period. (Courtesy of the School of Archaeology, Classics and Oriental Studies, University of Liverpool. Liverpool Museum 55.82.3.)

Chronology

The earliest boat models are Predynastic and are of pottery. From the Badarian Period, these roughly papyriform canoes are the earliest of all model types. Naqada I (Amratian) models are canoe-shaped, while Naqada II (Gerzean) and Naqada III boats are sickle-shaped, some with a high bow like the ships illustrated in the Hierakonpolis painted tomb 100 and on painted pottery. Archaic boat models are nearly all of ivory and seem to be predominantly papyriform (type III), some with raised bows and sterns like type V boats.

Wooden boat models appear to have originated in the Fourth and Fifth Dynasties at Saqqara and Gebelein, becoming more common in the Sixth Dynasty. These early boats have no crew, the earliest known model sailors coming from a Sixth Dynasty mastaba at Giza. It is not until the late/post Sixth Dynasty that boats regularly have crew.

The best-preserved Old Kingdom models are those from the pyramid of Queen Neith at Saqqara (figure 54). Comprising sixteen models, without crew, the flotilla includes types I, IV and V.

From the tomb of Meket-Re at Thebes came a fine flotilla of thirteen boats. Seven are type II boats used for personal transport, with items of luggage and furniture aboard. Two of these craft are kitchen tender

54. Type I Old Kingdom river craft with squared bows and sterns. Saqqara, pyramid complex of Queen Neith. Sixth Dynasty. (Cairo Museum. Photograph: Aidan Dodson.)

boats (models R and S) for long-haul travel requiring the provision of food (see figure 55). A smaller example, model X, was for sporting activities, such as fishing. The remaining craft are four type V pilgrimage boats and two type III skiffs (see figure 29). Meket-Re's type V boats have paddles and sails, but the majority of such models have not (figure 56). Painted tomb scenes indicate that ritual craft were usually towed to their destination.

During the Middle Kingdom, some type II river-boat models were used in funerals, equipped with a dais and canopy for the figure of the mummy and crewed by mourners. This is also the case for type IV boats in the late/post Sixth Dynasty and First Intermediate Period.

Type VI boat models are found only during the Twelfth Dynasty at el-Bersha and Lisht (figure 57). They are a peculiar hybrid form devoid

55. Type II kitchen tender boat carrying food supplies and a cook. El-Bersha, tomb of Djehutinakht. Late Eleventh or early Twelfth Dynasty. (Museum of Fine Arts, Boston 21.494. Photograph: Aidan Dodson.)

56. One of Meket-Re's pilgrimage boats, crewed by shaven-headed priests. Meket-Re himself sits under the canopy. Type V boat. Qurna, model U. Late Eleventh or early Twelfth Dynasty. (Cairo Museum JE 46716. From Winlock, *Models of Daily Life*, 1955, plate 46 bottom. Courtesy of the Metropolitan Museum, New York. Photography by the Egyptian Expedition, the Metropolitan Museum of Art, New York.)

of crew, but carrying the club and feather emblems and standards of several solar deities, including the Followers of Horus. The models from the tomb of Imhotep at Lisht have been described as the *mandjet* barque of the morning and *meskenet* barque of the evening.

From the New Kingdom are two models from the early Eighteenth Dynasty burial of Queen Aahotep at Dra Abu el-Naga. One boat is of gold with silver figures, the other entirely of silver. The former model has lotus-tipped finials, which gracefully curve inwards (type VII), while the latter resembles Middle Kingdom type II boats. The silver boat was originally found resting on a model wheeled carriage, which was one of the means used to transport boats around impassable sections of the Nile.

Whole models and parts of models have been found in the New

57. Type VI boat carrying the emblems of solar divinities. El-Bersha, tomb of Sepi III. Twelfth Dynasty. (Cairo Museum CG 4949. From Reisner, *Models of Ships and Boats*, 1913, plate XXII bottom.)

Kingdom tombs of Amenophis II and Tuthmosis III, but the only complete collection of boats comes from the tomb of Tutankhamun. It comprises thirty-five boats, most of which are of the simple travelling form, with two of type III, two type VII and four type V. The river craft form three flotillas based around the three larger state vessels. The two type VII boats have been described as barques of the sun and moon. The Twenty-first Dynasty tomb of the priests of Amun at Deir el-Bahri (Bab el-Gasus) contained a complete type VII wooden solar boat (figure 58).

Boat models can be used as a general dating tool. All type I models are Old Kingdom. Type IV boats with elongated end posts and double-stepped bipod masts date from the late/post Sixth Dynasty to the First Intermediate Period. A high stern angle in type II models is indicative of an early Middle Kingdom date, while a low angle and curled rudder fork indicate a Twelfth Dynasty date.

58. A type VII ceremonial boat with a closed cabin. The lotus flower finials are decorated with painted vignettes of Osiris and the solar barque. Bab el-Gasus cache at Deir el-Bahri. Twenty-first Dynasty. (Cairo Museum CG 4929. From Reisner, *Models of Ships and Boats*, 1913, plate XIX bottom.)

Purpose of model boats

Boat models allowed the tomb owner to travel the country; to cross from one bank to the other; to visit pilgrimage sites, such as Abydos, on festival days; to traverse the heavens and underworld in the company of the gods; and to make a safe passage from the land of the living (the east bank) to the land of the dead (the west bank).

Land transport

Overland transport for people was provided by a sedan chair. A unique model of Middle Kingdom date from Sedment depicts such a chair (figure 59).

Reliefs and paintings indicate that after the Second Intermediate Period

59. Unique representation of sedan chair bearers. Sedment, tomb 1525. Late Eleventh or early Twelfth Dynasty. (Courtesy of Manchester Museum. Object 6956a-e.)

persons of means travelled by chariot. There are no models of chariots, but a unique wooden model from Gebel Sohag of early New Kingdom date depicts a man on horseback. Its exact significance is uncertain.

Goods transported overland were carried on the backs of cattle and donkeys. The earliest model of a pack animal, a bull, comes from the tomb of Nyankh-Pepi-kem. Most Middle Kingdom models, however, are of donkeys driven on by a man wielding a stick.

House and home

Models of houses, their contents and the activities within, although few, are varied. The tradition of model houses and household furniture began in the Predynastic Period with a terracotta bed surrounded by a rail from Abu Zeidan, of Naqada III date, and a model house from el-Amrah. Two otherwise unique wooden models of a walled garden (figure 60), complete with copper-lined pool and detailed trees, are from the Middle Kingdom tomb of Meket-Re (models A and

60. View into a walled garden lined with trees. Note the amount of detail to the columns, and the copper rain spouts. Qurna, tomb of Meket-Re, model A. Late Eleventh or early Twelfth Dynasty. (Cairo Museum JE 46721. Photograph: Aidan Dodson.)

B). These residences are shown in great detail, including modelled doors with bolts, grilled windows and copper spouts for draining occasional rainfall from the flat roof.

Other models of houses exist, but in a different form. All of Middle Kingdom or later date, these soul houses, as they are called, are made of pottery. They range from simple huts to complex multi-storeyed buildings with rooftop terraces, some having domed silos (see chapter 4) and colonnaded façades. The courtyard of the soul house is filled with modelled food offerings comprising various types of bread, vegetables and meat, usually a haunch and head of beef. Drainage channels for libations are also present. Pottery offering trays which resemble these courtyards are another type of model. Both types were most commonly left above ground in a place accessible to the living, where a daily ritual could be performed for the dead. Models of houses continued to be made into the New Kingdom but lack the food offerings in the court.

The furnishings of the house are represented by the main item, the bed. Models of chairs are also known. Apart from providing comfort, it has been suggested that beds, in a mortuary context, relate to the fertility of the deceased (see below).

New Kingdom tomb paintings often depict a great banquet, with much eating, drinking and entertainment. Some of these activities are found as models. A unique model group from a Middle Kingdom tomb at Hu is of painted pottery (figure 61). It shows ten men, with outstretched arms, seated on low chairs around a low dining table laid with flat loaves, small cakes and racks of beef, and a stand containing two beer jars, one still sealed. In models of food production, eating is implicit: this model makes the activity explicit, as a banquet.

61. Handmade painted pottery models of people at a banquet found with a pottery soul house from which they may have come. Hu. Middle Kingdom. (Musées Royaux d'Art et d'Histoire, Brussels E.6273. Two further figures, Cairo JE 51347 and 51348 are not shown.)

62. Fine painted limestone harpist. Sheikh Farag, tomb SF 132. Middle Kingdom. (Cairo Museum. Photograph: Aidan Dodson.)

The entertainment of the deceased by harpists is first seen in the Old Kingdom. Three harpists, two female and one male, were among the figures from the Fifth Dynasty tomb of Nykau-Inpu at Giza. Several small limestone models of harpists, predominantly female, have come from Middle Kingdom contexts. One particularly fine male figure comes from Sheikh Farag (figure 62).

Wooden models of musical entertainment are also known. One example, from the Saqqara tomb of Karenen, shows the owner and his wife with a harpist on either side. In front of the couple are three women clapping and singing. A similar, though less detailed model is of two figures squatting on the ground facing each other (figure 63). The attitudes of their arms suggest that they may be singers, the woman shaking a *sistrum* in accompaniment.

The earliest dancing figure is from the late/post Sixth-Dynasty tomb of Nyankh-Pepi-kem. The naked girl stands with her feet together, her hair in three weighted braids on an otherwise shaven head. Possibly related to this figure are stone models of cavorting acrobats from tombs of the Middle Kingdom at Abydos and elsewhere.

During the Middle and New Kingdoms models of a type termed fertility figures, in wood, pottery, stone and faience, were placed in the tomb and these have also been found at domestic sites and in temple offering deposits. During the Middle Kingdom these female figures are depicted naked and without legs below the knees. Sometimes they are decorated with tattoos or wear a short beaded tunic of a type associated with dancers. Emphasis is placed on the genitalia, hence their association with female fertility. The New Kingdom figures are full-length and are often modelled lying on a bed next to a baby or a small child.

Dancing and its musical accompaniment are an important element of the worship of the goddess Hathor, patron of women, sexual love and childbirth. Depicting dancers and musicians in the form of tomb paintings, such as that of Mereruka seated on a bed next to his wife,

Egyptian Models and Scenes

63. Two figures, the
positions of whose arms
suggests that they may be
singers. Provenance
unknown. Twelfth Dynasty
(?). (Courtesy of
Manchester Museum.)

who plays the harp,
or as models of
musicians or as
votive fertility figures
would ensure for the
tomb owner not only
the possibility of new
heirs in the afterlife
but a safe rebirth into
it through the magical
properties of fertility figures and their association with Hathor. It is the
same potential for successful procreation, an important element in
Egyptian family life, that lies at the heart of simple model beds.

Models of people playing games are rare. One example, from Beni

64. Men aboard a sailing boat playing *senet*. Note the cow-hide shields and quiver. Beni
Hasan, tomb 186. Late Eleventh or early Twelfth Dynasty. (Courtesy of the School of
Archaeology, Classics and Oriental Studies, University of Liverpool. Ashmolean Museum,
Oxford. E. 2301.)

Hasan, shows two men on a boat playing a game of *senet* (figure 64). In a mortuary context, the game became a religious symbol for the deceased's endeavour to pass into the afterlife.

Household members included the wet-nurse. Figures of these women have come from the Nykau-Inpu Fifth Dynasty group, and from Middle Kingdom contexts figures of breast-feeding women in stone, faience and bronze.

There are also a number of unidentified tasks being undertaken by both Old and Middle Kingdom servant models. Other groups, such as boys and girls or men wrestling, are of uncertain purpose as models in a mortuary context.

Warfare

Until the reign of Sesostris III nomarchs maintained their own armed forces and fleets of armed ships. At certain times in Egyptian history the country was in turmoil: local economic failure caused by famine, combined with dynastic struggles, led to civil unrest. Such phases are termed Intermediate Periods. Symptomatic of such times of unrest are a series of models of soldiers and armed boats.

The earliest military model is of a fortified town wall, guarded by two soldiers. Made of pottery, it comes from a Predynastic grave at Abadiyeh.

Dating to the time before the reunification of Upper and Lower Egypt by Nebhepetre Mentuhotep II (before 2040 BC) are two battalions, each of forty soldiers, from the tomb of Mesehti at Asyut. One battalion depicts Egyptian soldiers and the other Nubians. Each figure is carved as an individual in height, facial features and shield design. Models of Nubian soldiers were also found in pit tomb 5, on the upper terrace of the tomb complex of Nebhepetre Mentuhotep II at Deir el-Bahri. Djehutinakht of el-Bersha had among his models a row of four marching Egyptian soldiers. The tomb of Nakhti at Asyut contained full-sized models of shields, bows, arrows and javelins in a quiver.

Unrest is also evident in the inclusion of weapons and soldiers on model boats from Beni Hasan and el-Bersha around the beginning of the Twelfth Dynasty (see figure 64).

Mourners

Reliefs and paintings indicate that figures of servants and family members in the guise of *djerty*-mourners represent Isis and Nephthys as the Two Kites during the funeral and burial process. These goddesses afforded protection to the mummy and ensured a safe passage to the afterlife.

Statuettes of the *djerty*-mourners appeared in stone and wood during the Old Kingdom. A boat model from Saqqara, with niches in its deck, indicates that mourners were originally placed on such models. Twelfth Dynasty funerary boats regularly depict the *djerty* at the head and foot of the mummy, arms outstretched in a protective gesture.

Other Middle Kingdom mourners appear as bell-shaped pottery figures, coarsely modelled, their hands held to their faces and heads as if weeping. The figures appear to have been made in pairs or sets of four, as one group from Asyut illustrates. Fragments of a finely modelled and painted pottery mourner appear to be unique.

A particularly fine pair of wooden figures of Isis and Nephthys, from the Twenty-first Dynasty tomb of the priests of Amun at Deir el-Bahri (Bab el-Gasus), depicts the goddesses with arms outstretched to protect the head and foot of the mummy (figure 65). They are bare-breasted and garbed in white skirts with red ribbons, the traditional attire of the mourner. From the late New Kingdom to Roman times figures of *djerty*-mourners have adopted a number of poses, from simply standing to kneeling with hands held to the face. These figures were probably intended to stand at the foot and head of the coffin both in the tomb and during its journey there by boat. Isis and Nephthys were also two of the midwife deities; their presence in the tomb would help usher the newborn deceased into the afterlife.

65. Figure of Nephthys as a *djerty*-mourner, her arms raised to protect the head of the mummy. Bab el-Gasus cache at Deir el-Bahri. Twenty-first Dynasty. (Cairo Museum JE 29264. Photograph: Aidan Dodson.)

7
Technology

The first servant models of the Predynastic Period were hand-modelled in clay or carved from pieces of ivory. The stone figures of the Old Kingdom vary greatly in size and quality: the later the model, the smaller and rougher its appearance. The carving of the bodily proportions tends not to follow the canon laid down for the representation of the human form. Some figures are so poorly modelled as to be barely recognisable (compare figure 66 with figure 19).

Similarly, the strictly frontal form observed in major statuary, such as that of the tomb owner, is lacking. Stone servant figures regularly have their arms and legs freed from the matrix in order better to convey the impression of activity. This is particularly evident in figures of millers and brewers.

Minor figures, such as servants, could be portrayed with physical deformities and ill-health, contrasting strongly with the ideal of healthy youth or well-fed maturity preferred for the tomb owner's statues.

Servant figures in stone were often poorly modelled. It has been suggested that apprentice masons were responsible for these figures, leaving the master masons free to concentrate on the tomb owner's figures. Whether servant figures are apprentice pieces or simply the result of careless carving remains unproven.

The stone used for these models is limestone, with the addition of sandstone and serpentine for New Kingdom examples. Models of food and food cases are either of limestone or calcite (Egyptian alabaster).

An increased sense of activity is seen in models made of wood. As in larger statues in wood, the limbs of servant figures could be freed from the body and a greater variety of positions achieved than was possible in stone. Late Sixth Dynasty wooden models, still mainly single figures, tend to be larger than their Middle Kingdom counterparts and are generally better made. The lack of accuracy and inattention to detail evident in models of all mediums did not detract from their inherent magical properties.

Wooden models were made from a variety of local and imported woods. The type of wood was chosen according to the degree of detail required. Indigenous trees included sycamore fig (*Ficus sycamorus* L.), acacia (*Acacia nilotica* Dest.) and tamarisk (*Tamarix nilotica* Ehrenb. and *Tamarix articulata* Vahl.). The lack of rain in Egypt resulted in relatively poor-quality wood, suitable only for certain cruder elements of model making. Imported finer-grained timber included the coniferous cedar and pine (probably *Cedrus libani* a. Rich. and *Pinus cedrus* L.).

The fine statuettes of servants carrying cosmetic jars of Eighteenth Dynasty date are of boxwood (*Buxus sempervirens* or *Buxus longifolia*). Analysis of the Meket-Re models has shown that for boat hulls and model walls not requiring detailed carving sycamore was used; its soft coarse grain tends to crack. The walls of the house models (models A and B), however, are of coniferous wood. The trees modelled in these gardens are sycamore figs. The figures of servants are of coniferous wood, as are mast steppings, rudders and the legs, ears, horns and tails of the cattle. In the carpentry shop (model J), the fixed post for sawing is of acacia, while the plank being cut is of fine imported coniferous wood. The mooring pegs and mallets on the boats are of tamarisk.

Analysis of other models has shown a wider variation. Sycamore has been used for walls, the bodies of figures, as bases and for boat hulls. Pine wood has been used for a similar range and also for the masts of boats and the legs of animal figures, while tamarisk was generally used for masts, rudders and oars. Although no formal analysis has been made of Tutankhamun's models, it is thought that at least one boat hull is of acacia.

The heads and bodies of wooden figures are carved in one, with arms made separately and attached with dowels, the join masked by a fine but thick gesso plaster (whiting and glue). It is clear, at least in the case of Meket-Re's models, that a stock of bodies was used, the attached arms alone determining what the figure's activity would be.

Feet on wooden models are either carved as one with the legs or made separately and pegged under the ends of the legs. An alternative was to terminate the legs in pegs which fitted into the base. The feet were modelled in plaster or simply painted on to the base.

For the el-Bersha Procession, the heads and bodies were made in one, with arms, legs, the fronts of the feet, and the priest's face made separately. Each figure carried something, and small elements of their loads were individually carved and joined together with dowels.

All parts of models, whether of stone or wood, were painted to supply details not carved, such as clothing and jewellery. Where paint has worn away, particularly on stone figures, the model appears very plain. Paint was made from naturally occurring plant and mineral pigments: carbon or lamp black (soot) and charcoal for black (hair, eyes, animal markings); iron oxide (possibly haematite) and red ochre for red (mainly male skin tones); yellow ochre for yellow (mainly female skin tones); gypsum (calcium sulphate) or chalk (calcium carbonate) for white (clothing); azurite or frit (calcium-copper silicate) for blue; and malachite for green. Where paint has eroded on wooden models, it is possible to see the white plaster used to render a smooth finish for painting. Meket-Re's models, once painted, were given a varnish of water-soluble gum, probably obtained from the acacia, lending a sheen to the surface. Wooden dummy vases from the tomb of Yuya and Thuya, in the Valley of the Kings at Thebes, have a resin varnish.

Though modelled fully clothed, many figures have, in addition, strips of linen torn from sheets tied about their bodies. Many models from Beni Hasan were modelled unclothed and then dressed in linen strips.

The bases for wooden models are often purpose-made, although examples are known where the base has been recycled, most often from a broken box with its joints and dowels still visible. A ploughing model, probably from Asyut, has as its base part of a coffin board bearing the offering formula, attesting to recycling even of those objects designed to last for eternity.

66. Very crude limestone miller. Note the stick-like legs and exceptionally crude modelling of the head and torso. Provenance unknown. Sixth Dynasty. (Courtesy of the British Museum, London. EA 2378.)

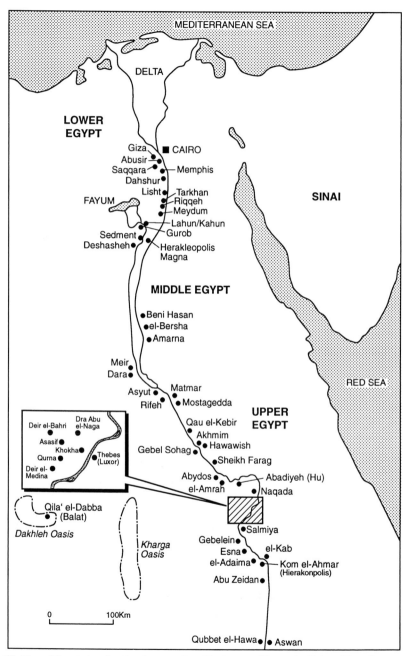

67. Map of Egypt showing the sites mentioned in the text. (Drawn by Robert Dizon.)

8
Further reading

Few works deal specifically with models. Articles, catalogues, museum guides and exhibition publications often contain entries about models.

Models, general

D'Auria, S.; Lacovara, P.; and Roehrig, C.H. *Mummies and Magic. The Funerary Arts of Ancient Egypt*. Museum of Fine Arts, Boston, 1988.

Borchardt, L. 'Die Dienerstatuen aus den Gräbern des alten Reiches', *Zeitschrift für Ägyptische Sprache und Altertumskunde* 35 (1897), 119-34.

Bourriau, J. *Pharaohs and Mortals. Egyptian Art in the Middle Kingdom*. Cambridge University Press, 1988.

Breasted Jnr., J.H. *Egyptian Servant Statues*. Pantheon Books, Bollingen Series XIII, 1948.

Garstang, J. *The Burial Customs of Ancient Egypt as Illustrated by the Tombs of the Middle Kingdom. 1902-4*. Archibald Constable, 1907.

Roth, A.M., and Roehrig, C.H. 'The Bersha Procession: A New Reconstruction', *Journal of the Museum of Fine Arts, Boston* I (1989), 31-40.

Winlock, H.E. *Models of Daily Life in Ancient Egypt from the Tomb of Meket-Re' at Thebes*. Harvard University Press, 1955.

Boat models

Belger, C. 'Deck, Ruderbänke und Mastbefestigung an ägyptischen Schiffsmodellen', *Zeitschrift für Ägyptische Sprache und Altertumskunde* 33 (1895), 24-32.

Boreux, C. *Études de nautique Égyptienne. L'art de la navigation en Égypt jusqu'a la fin de l'ancien empire*. Mémoires publiés par les membres de l'Institut Français d'Archéologie Orientale de Caire, 1925.

Glanville, S.R.K. (revised by Faulkner). *Catalogue of Egyptian Antiquities in the British Museum II. Wooden Model Boats*. British Museum Press, 1972.

Göttlicher, A., and Werner, W. *Schiffsmodelle im Alten Ägypten*. Arbeitskreis historischer Schiffbau e.V., 1971.

Jones, D. *Model Boats from the Tomb of Tut'ankhamun*. Tut'ankhamun's Tomb Series IX, Griffith Institute, Oxford, 1990.

Landström, B. *Ships of the Pharaohs: 4000 Years of Egyptian Shipbuilding*. Doubleday, 1970.

Poujade, J. *Trois flotilles de la VI ième Dynastie des Pharaons*. Centre de recherche culturelle de la routes des Indes, Gauthier et Villars, 1948.

Reisner, G.A. *Models of Ships and Boats.* Catalogue Général, Institut Français d'Archéologie Orientale du Caire, 1913.

Spanel, D.B. 'Ancient Egyptian Boat Models of the Herakleopolitan Period and Eleventh Dynasty', *Studien zur altägytischen Kultur* 12 (1985), 243-53.

Tooley, A.M.J. 'An Unusual Type of Model Boat', *Journal of Egyptian Archaeology* 72 (1986), 189-92.

Tooley, A.M.J. 'Boat Deck Plans and Hollow Hulled Models', *Zeitschrift für Ägyptische Sprache und Altertumskunde* 118, (1991), 68-75.

9
Museums

Most museums with an Egyptian collection contain one or two models, the following is a list of museums containing major collections of models and scenes.

United Kingdom
Ashmolean Museum of Art and Archaeology, Beaumont Street, Oxford OX1 2PH. Telephone: 01865 278000.
British Museum, Great Russell Street, London WC1B 3DG. Telephone: 0171-636 1555.
Fitzwilliam Museum, Trumpington Street, Cambridge CB2 1RB. Telephone: 01223 332900.
Liverpool Museum, William Brown Street, Liverpool L3 8EN. Telephone: 0151-207 0001.
The Manchester Museum, University of Manchester, Oxford Road, Manchester M13 9PL. Telephone: 0161-275 2634.
The Petrie Museum of Egyptian Archaeology, University College London, Gower Street, London WC1E 6BT. Telephone: 0171-387 7050, extension 2884.

Belgium
Musées Royaux d'Art et d'Histoire, Avenue J.F. Kennedy, 1040 Brussels.

Denmark
Ny Carlsberg Glyptotèk, Dantes Plads, DK-1550 Copenhagen V.

Egypt
Egyptian Antiquities Museum, Tahrir Square, Cairo.

France
Musée du Louvre, Palais du Louvre, F-75041 Paris.

Germany
Ägyptisches Museum, Staatliche Museen, Bodestrasse 1-3, 102 Berlin.
Ägyptisches Museum, Staatliche Museen Preussischer Kulturebesitz, Schlossstrasse 70, 1000 Berlin 19.
Ägyptisches Museum der Karl-Marx-Universität Leipzig, Schillerstrasse 6, 0-7010 Leipzig.
Roemer-Pelizaeus Museum, Am Stein 1-2, 3200 Hildesheim 1.

Italy
Museo Egizio, Palazzo dell' Accademia delle Scienze, Via Accademia delle Scienze 6, Turin.

Netherlands
Rijksmuseum van Oudheden, Rapenburg 28, 2311 EW, Leiden.

United States
Metropolitan Museum of Art, 5th Avenue at 82nd Street, New York, NY 10028.
Museum of Fine Arts, 465 Huntington Avenue, Boston, Massachusetts 02115.
University of Chicago Oriental Institute Museum, 1155 East 58th Street, Chicago, Illinois 60637.

Index

Page numbers in italic refer to illustrations